THE CLOUD MUSEUM

THE CLOUD MUSEUM

BETH SPENCER

SIXTEEN RIVERS PRESS

The Cloud Museum © 2018 by Beth Spencer

Printed in the United States of America

Sixteen Rivers Press
P.O. Box 640663
San Francisco, CA 94164-0663
www.sixteenrivers.org

Book, art, and cover design by author

Author photo by Antoine Baptiste

Library of Congress Control Number: 2017951983
ISBN: 978-1-939639-15-8

for Tony

Contents

Practicing Nowhere

The Book of Jay

PRACTICING NOWHERE

BY THE GATE

Sit down beneath the willow
dedicated to Alice of the open gate,
the siege, the parliament
of wings brightest in summer.
Sweet, the blood-red berries,
the road one longs to follow.

Sit down, sit down near the gate.
The robin has one ear to the ground,
the green snake flashes through
the grass. You must rest. Sharpen
your mind on the prospect
of nowhere.

Eggs rest in a nest, tiny
timpani whose casual movement
jars nothing. A neglected
errand, the desire to go on
like blue iris at the glistening
selvedge of marsh.

Here by the gate where Alice
rarely comes, children go on
with their play until fireflies
appear. Beneath the willow
sharpen your mind, your only mind,
on the prospect of nowhere.

THE BODY, SAID ALICE,

opening her shirt to show
her ruined breast, is ambivalent
with its laws. That's why we have two
of nearly everything. Before her,
a burning field, smoke building
puffy-headed fathers in the sky.
The braided cicatrix, her rattlesnake
tattoo ruddy in the light.

Will you stay awhile, I asked,
and rummaged for the wine,
but when I turned my back
she left again. The fathers nodded
on their sleepy stems. Across
the char her prints were off-
set dotted lines they couldn't bring
themselves to cut along.

Seven: The Devil Himself

The orphanage in flames, a nun with six
fingers on her left hand. Jars of library
paste, tubs for washing clothes.
These she remembers. More dimly

the father with a drinking problem,
the mother who preferred dolls to real
children. Alice slept in a dresser drawer,
later at the orphanage.

The nun would ripple a silver dollar
through her fingers. She taught Alice
the stations of the cross and how many crows
mean sorrow.

Fifteen years old, and the moon changing
over running fields. A train to Saskatoon.
When the conductor jingled his pockets,
Alice hoped it signaled a connection.

LIFELINE

I often fail Alice. It wearies
me to think of the ways.
Even more tiresome:
that she never notices,
has better things to do.

I am the smaller one,
a burr on her fleece,
a spur rolling after her boot.

When Alice plays her tambourine
and shakes her wild head
the building tips in on itself.
I chew my cuticle, sure
she will again be leaving.

She doesn't get it,
why I worry, even
that I worry. Imagine my hand
in yours, she once said. Imagine well
and what does it matter
if my fallible flesh is here
at all?

On stormy evenings, I touch
her callused fingertips,
the cold silver of her ring,
her lifeline flowing to the delta
of her complicated wrist.

HOMEOPATHY

Alice likes to go barefoot
much of the time.
A callus, she says, is many small injuries

become a shield
against true wounding.
Lightning in her odd-colored eyes

a coruscation that could sear
if you crossed her. Though *cross*
is not a word she cares for.

More sieve than sword she will listen hard
until you fall silent,
your armor rusting in the rain.

Eyes have their weather,
the breast its many sorrows.
Each fire, each loss

a small opening
so that as you move
there is less resistance.

EYES

The common buckeye has six,
three on each wing, the lower pairs
scanning to the side, the upper
straight behind. If I had wings
I'd add a fourth set, to watch
for Alice as I make my way
toward the horizon.
She has been evasive, her essential
strategy. She doesn't believe
in having. Alice says you never wind up
with what you thought you wanted.
The lover returns damaged,
needy. The cake in the window
tastes of dust. Once the book
is bound, it begins to die.
For happiness, she says, look at clouds,
and so I do. I take comfort
in their moods and colors
and how they let you forget for a while
the damned horizon.

En Garde

It falls to me then to slip
the spider's silk around my finger
like a ring or snare
and to keep my chin
down. Nothing but platitudes
occur to me when I am sad.
I mix them up to foil
myself: what doesn't kill you
lasts forever; nothing
makes you stronger. This, too,
shall perish; she who lives
by the sword shall pass.

Alice lives by the sword.
I pass my time imagining splendor
where there is none
and the spider swings through air,
diligent as God
but more dangerous.

ALICE IN THE WHEATFIELD

Ambivalence has its uses, she liked to say,
spreading her palms beneath the anvil clouds.
Bitter tea refreshes the palate, titrate of poppy
with cane stirs the senses. The hens dream
of stilted homes in paddies far
from the cats—each morning a fine egg,
a breakfast of grubs, a little grit.

Boots laced, Alice made for the horizon
decorated by lightning. I reject
porridge, but I do like fields, she said.
As for my companions, sweet thunderlings,
I deny them nothing. The abacus of pleasure
then becomes its opposite. In this way
we are all redeemed.

THE THUNDERLINGS, BULLETED

What I came to understand (I):

- They are invisible,
- her favored companions,
- ageless but not wise,
- negatively charged,
- beautiful as only outlaws can be,
- prone to disgruntlement.
  Alice learned their language the way
  one best learns any language, by living
  in the country where it is spoken.

What I came to understand (II):

- Alice finds them amusing,
- but did not choose them—
- they came to her.
  When?
  When, laughing, she showed
  her gold tooth. When she held out her hat
  for snow.

China Cup

Unfamiliar, the farms and houses
of the village, parapets askew, wires
crisscrossing the road.
Piglets, their tiny pink noses
through the slats, bring you around.
An old man in overalls spits
into the dust and you leave again,
toward the hollow this time.

Once you loved nothing more
than to listen to Alice and her thunder-
lings, but she is gone and they
have no one to follow. Listen as they
range along the horizon, random as potsherds,
aimless as thoughts
finally free.

Whatever you were sent to accomplish
you have forgotten. Your new project:
reinvention, as a small planet, perhaps,
with seas and moons, some
circumference, a path around the sun.
Or a china cup filling with sun,
a warmth to doze in,
you and your sawtoothed shadow.

LIKE BILLY THE KID, LIKE JESSE JAMES

Every move sets up a countermove.
In chess, in a life.
The sun wan as a day moon
over the garden. Alice is an outlaw.
She won't live among needlepoint homilies
and porch swings. All day I pruned the lavender
and roses, trained pea vines to the trellis.
I thought she might come for dinner.

She put my fingers through her hair.
So many snarls,
a little moisture near her temple.
I could feel her heartbeat there.
In the middle of her ear a small stirrup
for evasion, for not hearing me say
I wanted to go with her,

sleep outside under the receding moon
and the old white road favored by the dead.

SORTILEGE

She lived with other runaways
in an old house forgotten at the edge
of the city where they tangled
together at night to keep warm,
the prettiest bringing handouts
from café back doors.
During blizzards they covered the windows
with tarps and blankets, set fires
in the derelict stove. Smoke
merged cloudlike with the falling snow,
nothing anyone passing on the frontage road
would see. They played War
by firelight, read each other's palms.

When spring came, they scattered
in all directions, like the vowels of the Cree.
Alice found a boxcar, emptied
her pockets as it began to roll.
Each thing answered a question.
Why was she here? A black feather.
To whom should she answer? Chaff.
How long was the journey? A pebble
from the wild river, worn smooth.
Cigarettes were fallen columns
of places she had never been.
For days the fields passed by,
fallow, green, fallow, fallow, green.

PRACTICING NOWHERE

For the tanager, for the ground rose to bloom,
for the grapes to ripen. I wait for these. Meanwhile,
clouds, today a carnival, tents billowing blue
and gray and a shy green, midway ghosts leaning out
to spill secrets. Who are these wanderers?
The pewter edge of the future flashes, and laurel
leaves clap slender hands. Who am I?

> Early June, scaffold
> of regret collapsing—*boom!*
> Splintered, such beauty.

The great transformations are yet to come.
There is most joy when the outcome is least certain.
Blood carries this knowledge, leaps in the presence
of splendor. I was once magnetized by splendor but
feared it and numbed myself so as to tolerate
its presence. It had no choice but to leave.

> I carve a bamboo
> flute. The madness of the wind
> sings within me now.

What bird here in my hands? Fuzzy and crying,
awake for the first time. Later, a darkening,
the mother returned to feed, to warm and shelter.
To silence. Home as chafing dish.

> In the mirror, who
> is this aimless prodigal?
> Then fog, more clouding.

13

ROSEMARY

At dawn the finch shakes out the foil of his song
and the crow coughs matter-of-factly from the pine,
removing the sense I am here in any tangible way.
From the west some scrap of cloud,
like smoke or mist.
I count on these
since I cannot count on Alice.

Count on, as in scratching marks into the wall
of a cell.

Alice says time is relative, and I joke that
it's an uncle who is only kind when sober,
but I am not good with delivery,
my words swing like his damaged fist.

I drink coffee, spade the hardpan
so rosemary will grow. Devil's claw
is rampant here, and beggar's lice.
I water the rosemary by hand.
I have read it stands for fidelity,
keeps evil spirits from the door.

TRUST

I wait for the wind to blow
so that it does not,
my trust in outcomes

mostly thwarting them.
There is the field
burning and burning,

and underground the camas
that does not trust,
does not wait for spring

to come round again.
And spring returns
without fail.

THE BREAKS

For a gardener, she said, you are awfully wed
ded to specific out
comes. Tiny birds were in the sun
flowers, making lace of the leaves. Her
esy to Alice is knowing any
thing for certain. If a letter comes back post
age due, she rewrites it wholly, to
day's thoughts between yes
terday's lines, with many carets. Imp
ossible to parse without her draw
ings in the margins, her arrows and ad
diction to surprise pulling me a
long, giving me a way to under
stand.

Alyssum

Sweet alyssum. I sometimes say the name
when I am sad. For what do I grieve?
The mouse fear-frozen under a leaf
in my garden, the empty mouth of a bottle
making song in the wind.

Sweet alyssum, *worth beyond beauty*.
Alice tells me of the collision to come,
all beauty shattered on impact.
A comet, maybe a bomb, a coming together
of body and body.

Sweet asylum, my garden in spring,
blossoms of plum on needles
of pine. *Little cross*. Soon we will drink
to consecrate the season, the small green
snake a tendril round the stake.

BLUEBEARD

She saved the beard for last. So blue
it seemed like neon, sheen on a crow's wing,
the waves off Malibu.
Once upon a time, she liked to begin,
in America, possibly California . . .
before describing corpses locked in the secret
bloodstained room. Bodies first,
their scars, self-mutilations, teardrop tattoos.
Then the white face of the bride
and the key that wouldn't come clean.

He was proud of his whiskers,
like most of the cats around here.
She was altering the story,
buying the bride time
to extract a letter opener from the folds
of her gown. In her version, Bluebeard
wound up rotting on a meat hook,
his bones piling on the floor.

If you asked what happened to the bride,
she claimed not to know.
The bride got away.
That was enough.

HOLE

Open country, the little houses scattered
across a lake wide as the hereafter.
Onyx ice under the snow.
Inside each house, a hole, a small fire, whiskey.
Over each hole, a circle of men
smoking, passing a flask.
One line
strung between two worlds.
Once, the bell tinkled and the men groaned,
but it was nothing.
On the hook, a bit of flesh
that in the firelight was shiny and pale.
Only chum.
She had been to see her father.
Oh, you can't imagine how cold it was,
she said, shaking the crystals out of her hair.

ROPE TRICKS

Alice was practicing rope
tricks high in the barn.
The mule snorted when her loop
shimmied down his neck,
chickens scattered like jacks
from her whip crack.

I was inside the house watching tornados
on YouTube: Fargo, Joplin,
Manitoba. How the earth
reached up, lifted a chalice
they danced inside.

Summer was passing into fall,
the well was nearly dry.
I added another finger to my glass
and fiddled with the volume.
Alice leaned out of the hayloft,
lassoing an early storm.

RAIN

Mazy paths a madwoman could love, lightways
running between the clouds.

Muddy river, fish snagged in the barbed
wire of low-lying fences,

and shingles of the houses
trying to lift, singing at the gutters.

In yards, tiger lilies wanting more
and harder, and again, more.

ALICE UNDERGROUND

The thunderlings object, fret the sky blue-
black with their grumbling. Outlaws
loving only their own flash and physics.
But Alice doesn't fear collision or sparking

or circuit breakers blown to hell.
Or the underground.
The coldest place in the cosmos lies
under our feet, says Alice.

Alice: a cathedral
of intersecting forces, a field
of crows flying the cross-
winds. Threatening

sabotage, the thunderlings
have my sympathy for once, their crazed
harangue masking their fear
of losing her to the unknown.

Do they mean to drop breadcrumbs,
tempt her back to the horizon?
Or blister the long flight
of steps leading down into darkness?

WORD

They knew.
They hunched into it.
Word was coming from somewhere
and crows were lined up on the wire
near the wheatfield.
When word came from across
the county the river the sea
I saw her brave body splayed,
its ink already dry.
Telephone poles leaned in,
wooden heads crowded
with word, forgotten
lines swagged in the weeds.
Word came down
or up from, we say,
or from across.
Word came.

Escape Hatch, Flickering Field

Things were waking, crying, struggling
to get free. Crackling, blood, shell
confetti, clouds running over the wheatfield.
Some darker business high in the sky, anvil
or fist, and through the grasses
silken whispering,
restless, susurrant.

The fence needed wire, the gate
sagged open. In the hole
the hook had fallen from, two small eyes
looked out.

There is no world more terrible,
a voice said. And then,
softer than the voice,

rain.

THE BOOK OF JAY

To create a little flower is the labour of ages . . .

—Blake

mirage

toward the end
                a sort of baptism
         cloud of road dust
barely recalled yellow summer hills
                        a boy's glance a flame a hand a jaw
                        bone in the draw
   cathedral of dust following father's car
                     through depression towns
    i could block out the rest
                angry words
                    rotten fruit
                        heat its own law
through haze sometimes the mountain
         i was thirsty i needed something to drink
                        maybe a mountain
                        cool with snow
                        a river   yes some water a cool plum
            a sunny apricot would do
                     wasps drifting long-legged
                     over the windfall
car towing its church through the shadows
                        then light a shaft a black hole
            sometimes a whole wing
                            santos de polvo rising again
          an arm swept across a brow
                        men in rows bent
                        to short hoes
                        a hundred suns through straw
   i felt what i saw
                     open mouths of birds in blue twilight
                        their great wheeling flight

a gypsy could say how tall this horse stands the bay that someone maybe my grandfather has laid me atop in my diaper and cotton shirt my fingers in its ropey mane shiny dark animal with gentle eyes no one else in the picture that's how gentle who does that with a baby 1929 my mother's parents' place dirt floor no plumbing no electricity you might say i got my funk on at an early age under cobalt skies the black forest behind us i have a large head don't you think the better to hold two worlds this one wild the other tame my father's parents' san francisco home with maid i wonder what all was in my mind here scent of horseflesh hilly warmth of spine someone out of the frame murmuring good good good was it mother behind the tripod wearing a hood i can almost feel a shiver in the coffee-colored hide

ground to withers sixty inches
fifteen hands in gypsy speak

father away in california
ten years before their divorce

conductor

making slows time
i was a lonely kid
art was a world i could control
sort of

always on a tightrope
apollo v dionysus
one exhausted me with perfection
the other let me wander drunk
on the nectar of uncertainty

flickering alembic
classical | primitive
city | country
goggles & tripods | mirrors & stars
well-lit studio | darkroom
figural | abstract

i ran on alternating current
it helped me hold a charge

alum rock park

a long painting
puts you in the god seat
i mean in the best way also the worst
you're creating the world then if you're me often
as not destroying it so you can rebuild it the next day
everything goes into it the butterfly sipping mineral salt from
a rock along penetencia creek the day i kissed the mexican boy

alum rock park 1945
geologic miracle pardon
the redundancy a steaming canyon
where did i lay the sable brush the look
in his eyes light on the water behind him smell
of sulphur in the grotto you add bits of mica to the paint
regroove a glinting ray coming through the west bay window

there's
a sparkle
he's tipping
my face toward his
my friends are laughing
on the bridge i hear them
in the distance what was his name

he was
something i tried
for weeks to find a way to draw
it wasn't alum but i think the word
has taken hold in me alum working its spell
i alum-knife another ridge smooth it with my cloth
my dress was blue it was may butterfly moving its wings
slowly on the rock a consecration my breast warming under his hand

bird on a wire

i i
wanted
to create a work
that was just so precariously
balanced
between going this way
or that way
that it maintained
itself

spain

sometimes i dream of the eye
of the bull which of course i couldn't see
from where i sat but no matter
there was a glint in the night of it
when he faced the cape
red not to anger him
but to mask the blood
when the matador plunges his blade
between the heaving shoulders
i preferred the verónicas
man and beast sizing each other up
the man holding the cape like a curtain
like the piece of cloth saint veronica handed
to christ on his way to golgotha
that he might wipe his bloody brow
below the weight of his cross

the beast trots past it
the languorous sweep it makes
before the man pivots and who doesn't think then
of the death to come
and the severed ear of the bull in hemingway
that romero gives lady brett

i was trying with my palette knife
to capture the flourish of the cape
that loveliness and grace
and its opposite the eye going dark
the cry unanswered

painterland equations

they call it frailing
a kind of bump-diddy beat

meanwhile

frailing ≠ fretting
instead a fine fettle
always in jazz time the boys
in the band the endless party

most nights

one two + one two
+ one more before bed
we were young you know
it was how we all lived then

every night

band practice + traffic sounds
poetry + paint
the pearly plastic inlay
called oh yes "mother of toilet seat"

nevertheless

my rose + more rose ≠ morose
i entered that fleur + it me
i lowered the seat
not to fall in the bowl

it is true

they thought my flower =
a kind of madness
though they admired it too
at least my passion for it

all art

is madness anyway all of us trying
to solve for some crazy x

an apron shape no less no doubt a nod to how i mock-
mothered the men in that place though some would
say not an apron a smock ok but with a smiling nude
right about here she sort of resembles me her tits
are bigger but not by much he wasn't a doda man
might have been his kansas childhood he liked his bad
girls on the good side we were art compañeros when
mcclure told me about him said he was coming west
i had dreams of his paintings crates of them arriving
but it actually happened trunks of them showed up
at mike's even before he did you had to love the guy
who else would have come up with the rat bastard
protective association the rbpa for short a neo-
pre-raphaelite brotherhood only with women in it me
and dear joan brown she at least looked pre-raphaelite
look here's a tap-dancing diagram we did tap each
other for ideas he liked my nylon stockings filled
with xmas gifts and hanging from the ceiling for one of
our better parties looks like one of my amber drop
earrings here
and
lower
a zipper, a sort of queen card
then something shabby
dangling
a
very
long
tail

color wheel

i made my own you know you can't discount jazz the clubs were hopping one night i caught basie's eye he asked me backstage to run away with him one o'clock jump there paris had a soft light a blueness about the atmosphere—oh & the crumbling walls i came into my own as an abstract expressionist everything i ever made a portal or eye into the very tissue of falling columns to work—a rose window if you will containing everything trying endlessly to get the shape just right—impossible! i must have drawn a thousand wheels i formed a circle to go into to see how i would do & i never really left

tongue-tipped furnace pollen

the poet from wichita called my white rose

also
a yogic breath held for five years
a dream of sweat in shape of petal
a veronica. a pure gesture
a perfumed thorn and spiked blossom
a damp cameo of hips and rage and smiles and velvet

he couldn't separate me from my painting he said
we all loved her he said

also
that he thought too much about my arms

double harrow

there was a wall we worked on opposite
       sides but i was the more unsure
each day looking at her canvas
       and she at mine
one of us working a shape
       up in the high right corner
and the other
       it is hard to believe
the same shape
       or close enough it was as if
we worked from a single notion
       though now thinking back maybe
we weren't as alike
       as it seemed at the time it was peculiar
though and i got frightened a little i can say that
       i mean it wasn't just painting we would go
out and without knowing what
       the other was doing come back
with the same pair
       of shoes something like that
when she left town
       i admit it i felt a great release
you see it wasn't always
       a friendly thing it scared me how she would walk in
at day's end and say this is good this is sub par
       and i believed her
almost always and sometimes even painted
       out what she said was not as good
you may say ridiculous yes of course but

years later i had a show in new york
she sent a petition around saying i had stolen
all my ideas from her
when i paint now sometimes i wonder
what she is doing on the other side
of the country i hope she is still working
i hope she is not dead

critic

if an artist is a person *besieged*
by unstable forces what is a critic
if not someone outside the force field
no one could possibly know a work's entire
provenance though it is the job
of the critic to give it context a place
to hang

his first review felt like a beheading
here she is world here's what she's about
and here's a fart a farthingale
we talked about it later he became dear
here's the thing an artist cannot stop making
for long i was if anything galvanized
i stepped up my game
swung harder watched the ball dis
appear a star
spica perhaps but that is how i work

in my playbook the giants
smoke the dodgers every time

not endless

not a road not a thousand roads
not one point of convergence not the ladder
sheathed in paint not the cat watching me work
or the billowing fog
its blue petticoats
not occasional truck thunder not water
hammering the pipes not bobby singing
how does it feel because i tell you it felt pretty good
most days i did not walk the via negativa
but tripped the light monastic my rose
neither prim nor wild
attracting pilgrims who shared cigarettes and wine
and stared at her
while i added or scraped off layers

raked by headlights after dark she almost seemed
to breathe one night a bat got in
crawled across her before flying
over the bed then out the window
i imagined its mouth
on the lead-laced petals its small face
brushing the paint
it made me sad
it was as if i too were small before my fleur
not knowing where she planned to lead me
after fillmore street after we moved
have you ever seen a bat's foot
so like its hand
in the morning i could just make out
where it had made its mark

the wise & foolish virgins

if there is something i resist
it's sentiment it ruins art
i'm not talking about tenderness
or love that makes work possible but a mawkish
attachment to symbols that leaves a hangover
a sluggishness as from a sugar crash
please don't go on about *the soul* to me
unless you admit its entire gamut
gamete to maggot

in the parable the wise virgins
kept their lamps trimmed and burning
but their foolish sisters ran out of oil
the lord swept in while they were looking to resupply
point being they missed their holy bridegroom
but could a case not be made for what they learned
from their broken hopes how grief sharpened
their senses imagine marriage to god give me
a little serpent any day i thought as i painted
rose after rose after rose i threw all of them out but two
i guess that was somewhat lordish of me
but they reeked of tearstain an addiction to sorrow

i wanted something more
las rosas mysticas
i wanted you to enter them like a bee
become lost in their scent and textures
not be able to say
which one is foolish
which one wise

love can be stupid i'll give you that but I'd like to set the record straight on me and wally and his notions about funk when we met i had this little house on magnolia but i was playing around with plaster huge works and the place was often a mess he was always starving never had enough money for food he began coming around partly for the meals you understand but we were falling for each other so i was trying to take a little more care not too much though i was serious about my work wally understood that much knew that a muse demands fealty when she shows up you get to work you don't get out the vacuum or do your laundry she'd walk right back out one afternoon he calls says he's on his way over it's getting to be suppertime of course i hadn't showered for a few days my clothes were all over the floor plaster bits everywhere oh shit oh well the hamper was full but the fridge was empty i just grabbed all my underwear and shoved it in there trying to buy myself a little time at some point i leave the room and he goes to check out the fridge no doubt hoping i'll ask him to stay for supper guess he was pretty shocked but i didn't expect him to tell the smithsonian years later it was but one example of my essential funkiness he said the fridge wasn't even plugged in maybe it wasn't i don't remember but if not so what i should have just hauled my panties and whatnot out of it right then and worked them into a piece called *wally misses the whole goddam point of being an artist*

time pure flowing falling wing
breton & lamantia

sounding sibyl I am watching you
          materia immateria that may well scratch
x in the rue notre-dame-de-lorette
          the stone caught in long stockings
the earth rolled out over the watergrown precipice
          a swarm of nothing and the sun
two lovely crossed legs
          in silken laddersnakes of tau
head flaring out over the door of the unknown room
          always for the first dancing vibratories
the snake flies blueskimmed grade of the night
          the fascinating rift occurring and transvectisizing
heart stars heart stars heart stars
          before me o time pure flowing falling wing
riding cantilever swarm back in
          hardly do i know you on temporal levels
a wholly imaginary cosmogonic signature
          in the facade at first you coalesce stipple air
the elusive angle of a shaman it's a field
          of jasmine fire unlocking by a frenzy
all the flowers your presence
          passed into the future
tau always for the first time

44

howl

o rose
said his beloved blake
thou art sick

o america
said allen's poem
its throat open to the moon

eyes

three pairs of owl-eye windows next door
made me laugh   i imagined birds
two stories tall installed by   say   huac to spy
on us everyone here a poet or artist
you know   dangerous
i was drawing eyes then
maybe mine   very very large
if j. edgar's birds were watching
dammit i would watch right back
i was almost 30   never could guess
what was coming next   i just drew and drew
lashes brow hairs and when the eyes got too spooky
verticals a kind of screen
at night the owl eyes glowed   the birds stone silent
not like the colorado owls
of my youth all night calling *hoo-hoo-hoo*
i didn't draw in pupils   wanted a fortune-teller stare
two crystal balls
what did they see   the rose probably
when   years on   a vandal bent on the cyclopic
defaced one eye
i worked through my grief drawing rounds
their record shape a nod to basie
one o'clock jump   i was past
the midpoint of my life   the stones
had a hit that summer   miss you
a lot of *oo-oo-oo*
i kept time with the count
i drew and drew

bodice for a funky girl

here it all comes
here is the bodice of love splayed
my last valentine faceted
the tender waist the spreading
hips arrayed the other side
of the eternal pivot point the spindle
there it all goes eternal parade
it never ends the closing down
the opening up again times twelve
houses of the zodiac four seasons
of the deck or endless fashioning

some places i worked not counting inside my head
pensione bartolini in florence
magnolia st. berkeley
cobblestone kitchen across the bay
painterland on fillmore where i cloistered
with my flower eight years my big mudpie
pasadena for a spell of touching up
while breaking up

then no work
the hedony of marin
before i got back to it
i faced mortality open-mouthed
always i suppose i set some kind of bad example
wally told the interviewer
but he should know a swamp
is only the best place to cast for what
we bury then after a time bear forth

deathrose

not throes my friends
don't be so eager
to pitch me in the myth bin
for tortured artists
yes there was lead in the paint
and later five of my teeth fell out
but i got a bridge
i'm also getting ahead
of my story

it's true i scraped that flower to death
at least four times
and painted her back
would have kept on working
if the rent hadn't gone up

the bekins men were real pros
wrapped my rose in blankets
like a secret lover
she was big weighed over a ton
they had to saw the window
larger to get her out

down she went in her custom coffin
me smoking in the void
she left behind

ask bruce he got it all on film
i love him dearly but that day he read a bit too much
thanatos into my eros

the split

    along the fault line houses shudder every tremor
    each crack teaching me how fast time passes i track
    my own passage in cloud-filled windows ash trays
    empty cans of housepaint the ache in my gums i have worn
    my soles down climbing city hills there should be a path
    a way to hollow through the fog to southern european sun

    we're breaking up
                evicted
                        moving the art to a barn

           still
                  i'd say we had a pretty good run

crescent bridge

one life gave way to another strange
　　　　　how that bridge came to stand
for what i'd left as much as for
　　　　　a whole new world like oz in green
fantastic glory after years of gray
　　　　　fog washing in and out of the city
traffic noises sirens banjo madness
　　　　　the fraught funk of a marriage gone
sad my rose in exhibition limbo it's no surprise
　　　　　i lost five teeth the wonder of it
was the repair my own re-pairing too
　　　　　sometimes everything is metaphor
when i was sorrowing everything was teeth
　　　　　stone outcropping at drakes bay
near the lighthouse even the cycle of the cove itself
　　　　　its coming and going i got my teeth
back and a camera an aperture
　　　　　a brand new eye to document
the change the way when you come north across
　　　　　the golden gate there's a tunnel
you pass through the darkness of the underworld
　　　　　then *shazam* the glory of marin
wolfback ridge mt. tam ablaze with paintbrush
　　　　　of all things and toothwort too
one day i threw the tarot my crossing card the bridge
　　　　　the five of wands
my teeth i thought
　　　　　i did a lot of ruminating then
a word for thinking
　　　　　also chewing

a cake for janis

i don't remember what kind
something gooey probably with nuts and butter
cream for the young queen of the blues
new to the neighborhood
someone else the matrons of marin
could worry would corrupt their kids

we were prime
for a time neither of us guessing
how quickly the parties
the beautiful boys
could ruin us for work
but janis liked to say you can destroy
your motherfucking now
by worrying about tomorrow
and please pass the tequila

we drank through a sunrise or two
in her tripped-out porsche
as for mercedes benz
three days after she recorded it she died

o janis o lord
when she opened her door
i saw those startled blue eyes
and dropped that cake *crash*
on her porch

my pendulum heart beating jazz time
between the monumental
and the microscopic
momentum baby momentum
it was a question of accommodation
vistas and visitations
also art supplies i was arrested once
for stealing paint lost my job
over two cans one red one black
kept it from my parents though
damn in canada artists get government aid
i don't know if that's good or bad
but at least there's less money for war
paint isn't cheap not when you need a lot of it
i made jewelry for a while out of oddments
used an ice pick and tweezers it sold well
but the imp was in my blood
saying go large again make something
of yourself i always did try
get out your magnifier you'll find bits of me
and my dogs in almost everything
i painted or shot did you ever see my photos
of r. mutt's cast it's all right there
his swinging gait   the break   the midpoint cast
then afterwards him trotting along again
my midpoint happened in ross
that long hush after *the rose*
when the record ran out white noise *shhhhhhhhhh*
and i went small again

salvador dalí's birthday party

he wasn't there of course but i imagined him
the catalan master on his 69th
hovering over my little larkspur house
with barebreasted gala his wife both of them
cheering *sí sí sí* my reckless pour
of darkroom fluids across papers i tipped in and out
of the light here are the candles or are those flames
we were celebrating him but also
the persistence of me

and his mustache
look here it almost is
or a woman with a penis gala says
that's us *querida* says snidely salvador
time to blow out the candles says i make a wish
myself i wish for the war to end
and a bigger studio

i was full of joy the government had just dropped
its charges against ellsberg maybe those flames
were exclamation points
sí sí sí

on the radio war blasting cisco kid i tell you
we were having quite the fiesta
salvador gala and me
ay ay ay

i made 20 prints that day

disappearing artist

when the handle of your knife
dries & pulls away from the blade
here's a fix a cup of water
will swell the wood

sometimes it's best to go under
for a while not into abasement
but the shadows of a kelp forest
let your jazzy doppelgänger
ply the life raft above
pay the rent teaching

become a disappearing artist
tighten your groove
when your edge returns make time
shoot everything the netted breakdown couch
the fan acanthus dew-dropped cabbage leaf
your dental bridge
look forward back
your dear rear window athwart a slant incision

a few strings to periphery
wick wisdom's ambiguity
what a slosh of day & night
what pink immortal intimate
something plain to drink from
a simple fired cup

her gait

there was a horse i sometimes dreamed of
running through my head at night
i thought of her as my horse sense
dark and bright at once
coffee in an earthquake
tearing up the track or maybe one
of my endless circles
i tell you she left every other racer
choking on her stardust
if my rose was *a fact painted somewhere*
on a slow curve between destinations
she was a great flashing stroke
in a painting by kline that kind of wild
once i dreamed her on an ice floe
drifting out to sea not panicked
though her mane made furious lace
in the wind where is she going i wondered
when i woke someone had the paper
there was a story about a filly
who blew out her front leg in a race
they put her down i couldn't read any more
went outside walked around
it was one of those cold summer days
no sun everyone looked half dead
a leaded window down the street
some girl's bedroom
between the glass and curtain a line
of toy animals a black pony high-stepping
spurred me home to work

september blackberries

i have been thinking of you
my friend
have made you a bright offering
of my teeth

not leonine but sharp enough

in september
when the berries are ready
see how the cougar steps
among the canes

carefully

to take one
she is curious
she is lactating
all her *mad cubs* denned

and dreaming

the berry is more tart
than those in the gut
of the deer
cached for later

then
such fine gnashing

dove one

once again the eye a mystery i placed
at the center of my painting though whose
mine or the dove's i leave for you to parse
i will tell you this the bird was unafraid
it seemed to know i was trying to save it
also that its life was going
did it look back then to the nest of twigs and roots
it fledged from did it feel fear
the first time it flew
or swoon into the falling
only try its wings by accident
then join its tribe rejoicing
i recalled the doves of florence
their iridescent fluttering
a sound like shuffled cards
or peace accords
i watched its eye lose light
it seemed there was an opening
where sky and ground were one i fell in
watched the field shift to infinite
i liked how my brush felt feathering
the linen and how the eye
bright with oil carried in it something
of the way a life can quicken for a time
and more slowly come to rest

dream/rückenfigur

a museum not sure which one
maybe the whitney i saw no one i knew
i'm walking through the rooms
yet see myself among the paintings
as someone else a visitor
young again my unruly hair
not lost to chemo
she has my eye and sense of style
my passion for chiaroscuro

we round a corner
and there it is my fleur
in a dark alcove lit from the sides
and this is the truth it is like seeing
her for the first time radiant
timeless perfectly restored
all the grime washed off
a few mica flecks glinting

we stand there taking her in breathing
a scent of something
not the wine or cigarettes of fillmore street
maybe the wild roses of tamalpais
then somehow i am separate again

feeling a little cocky i approach my double
whisper into her hair *you know*
i did that

NOTES

THE BOOK OF JAY

The poems in this section are in the voice of American artist Jay DeFeo (1929–89). Many liberties were taken.

"mirage": Jay DeFeo's last painting, *Mirage*, is suffused with yellow and gold. As a child during the thirties, she traveled the migrant camps of Northern California with her father, a physician.

"colorado primitive": DeFeo's mother's parents, with whom young Jay spent several summers, lived a hard-scrabble life in Colorado.

"alum rock park": This park, on the east side of San Jose, California, is near where DeFeo lived as a teen. By then, its heyday as a spa with hot springs had passed, though parts of grottos and other ruins remained.

"bird on a wire": The poem is a verbatim statement by DeFeo to art historian Paul Karlstrom. Oral History Interview with Jay DeFeo, 3 June 1975–23 Jan 1976. Archives of American Art, Smithsonian Institution, Washington, DC.

"spain": After college DeFeo spent more than a year in Europe, taking in a bullfight while in Spain. Later she painted *The Verónica*.

"color wheel": The italics are from John Muir. DeFeo used them to title two of her paintings. The phrase in the innermost circle is loosely taken from Blake's "If you have form'd a Circle to go into, go into it yourself & see how you would do." DeFeo loved the music of Count Basie; at one of his San Francisco shows he reportedly asked her to run off with him.

"*tongue-tipped furnace pollen*" and the other quotations are from a poem about Defeo's most famous painting, *The Rose,* by poet Michael McClure, who gave the name "Painterland" to the house at 2322 Fillmore, San Francisco, that he shared with DeFeo; her husband, Wally Hedrick; and others.

"double harrow": DeFeo and painter Sonia Gechtoff lived in adjoining apartments at Painterland. The poem quotes and riffs off comments DeFeo made to art critic Paul Karlstrom about their odd, often troubling relationship.

"critic" includes a nod to Rebecca Solnit's statement about cities; it also references art critic Thomas Albright, DeFeo's mixed-media work *White Spica,* and her love for the San Francisco Giants. Spica is the name of a blue giant in the constellation Virgo.

"the wise & foolish virgins": DeFeo named this pair of paintings after a watercolor by William Blake in his *Songs of Innocence and of Experience.* Dana Miller, *Jay DeFeo: A Retrospective* (New York: Whitney Museum of American Art, 2012–13).

"*time pure flowing falling wing*": The poem alternates lines from André Breton's "Always for the First Time" with those from an untitled poem by Philip Lamantia that DeFeo taped to the back of her drawing *Eyes.*

"bodice for a funky girl" takes its cues from DeFeo's painting *Last Valentine* and comments her husband made to Paul Karlstrom. Oral history interview with Wally Hedrick, June 10–24, 1974, Archives of American Art, Smithsonian Institution. "A Little Misunderstanding" draws from the same comments.

Deathrose was DeFeo's initial name for *The Rose*. Her friend, artist Bruce Conner, filmed it being moved out of Painterland, adding a somber commentary.

"crescent bridge" is a large painting DeFeo did of her dental bridge after she moved to Marin following the breakup of her marriage.

"a cake for janis" is based on a story reported by Paul Liberatore in "Lib at Large: An artist's celebrated obsession comes home," *Marin Independent Journal*, December 10, 2012.

"salvador dalí's birthday party" references an eponymous set of photographs in which DeFeo experimented freely with darkroom chemicals and various exposures.

"her gait" addresses DeFeo's admiration for the paintings of Franz Kline in the context of an imagined dream. She wrote her friend Wallace Berman that "the White Rose is a Fact painted on a slow curve between destinations. This is all I remember and this is all I know."

"september blackberries" is for Michael McClure.

"dream/*rückenfigur*" recounts a dream DeFeo had toward the end of her life.

Acknowledgments

Huge thanks to the editors of the following journals, in which these poems first appeared or are forthcoming:

Cutthroat: "The body, said Alice," "Lifeline," "Practicing Nowhere," "Alyssum"
Iron Horse Literary Review: "Seven: The Devil Himself"
Antithesis: "color wheel"
Empty Mirror: "mirage," "spain," "not endless," "the wise & foolish virgins," "eyes," and "disappearing artist"

I am happy the following poem first appeared here as a letterpress broadside:

Quoin Collective: "Word"

Many thanks to Joanne Allred, Jeanne Clark, and Josh McKinney for early feedback on these poems. Thanks also to artist Leslie Mahon-Russo for her comments on the Jay DeFeo part of the manuscript. An affectionate shout-out to my former poetry professors, George Keithley and Gary Thompson. Bear hugs to Foxfire and all the Coots, and a roar of appreciation to the Bear Stars, whose work has been a huge inspiration for over twenty years. Big love to my parents, Donald and Dorothy Spencer; my brothers, Lee and Paul; and especially to my husband, Antoine Baptiste. Finally, much gratitude to all the good people at Sixteen Rivers Press for their helpful advice on these poems, their commitment to poetry, and for publishing this book.

About the Author

BETH SPENCER was born in Portland, Oregon, and has lived in several other states as well. After working too many jobs to count, she founded Bear Star Press, which publishes poetry and short fiction by writers in western states. She lives in rural Northern California with her husband and dog. *The Cloud Museum* is her first book.

Sixteen Rivers Press is a shared-work, nonprofit poetry collective dedicated to providing an alternative publishing avenue for Northern California poets. Founded in 1999 by seven writers, the press is named for the sixteen rivers that flow into San Francisco Bay.

SAN JOAQUIN • FRESNO • CHOWCHILLA • MERCED • TUOLUMNE
STANISLAUS • CALAVERAS • BEAR • MOKELUMNE • COSUMNES • AMERICAN •
YUBA • FEATHER • SACRAMENTO • NAPA • PETALUMA